HIP-HOP
Biographies

PITBULL

MW01535363

SADDLEBACK
PUBLISHING

HIP-HOP Biographies

Chris Brown

Drake

50 Cent

Jay-Z

Nicki Minaj

Pitbull

Rihanna

Usher

Lil Wayne

Kanye West

SADDLEBACK
P U B L I S H I N G
www.sdlback.com

Copyright © 2013 by Saddleback Educational Publishing. All rights reserved. No part of this book may be reproduced in any form or by any means, electronic or mechanical, including photocopying, recording, scanning, or by any information storage and retrieval system, without the written permission of the publisher. SADDLEBACK EDUCATIONAL PUBLISHING and any associated logos are trademarks and/or registered trademarks of Saddleback Educational Publishing.

ISBN-13: 978-1-62250-015-4
ISBN-10: 1-62250-015-6
eBook: 978-1-61247-696-4

Printed in Guangzhou, China
NOR/1112/CA21201417
17 16 15 14 13 1 2 3 4 5

Table of Contents

Timeline

1981: On January 15, 1981, Armando Christian Pérez was born.

1985: Armando's parents divorce.

1995: Armando starts selling drugs.

1997: Armando's mother throws him out of the house.

1998: Pitbull meets hip-hop producer Irv Gotti.

2001: Luther Campbell signs Pitbull to a one-year contract.

2003: Pitbull's rap song "Oye" is part of the *2 Fast 2 Furious* soundtrack.

Lil John puts "Pitbull's Cuban Rideout" on his album, *Kings of Crunk*.

Pitbull signs a contract with TVT Records.

2004: Pitbull releases his first album, *M.I.A.M.I.: Money Is a Major Issue*.

2005: Pitbull, Sean "Diddy" Combs, and Emilio Estefan form Bad Boy Latino Records.

2006: Pitbull's father dies.

Pitbull releases his second album, *El Mariel*.

2007: Pitbull releases his third album, *The Boatlift*.

2009: *Rebelution*, Pitbull's fourth album, is released.

2010: Pitbull puts out a Spanish-language album, *Armando.*

2011: Pitbull's album, *Planet Pit*, is released.

2012: Pitbull goes on a world tour.

Pitbull releases *Global Warming*, his seventh album.

Pitbull's Cuban Heritage

Fans of rapper Pitbull may call him "Mr. 305." The number stands for the area code for the Miami, Florida, area. Pitbull was born in Miami. But to really understand Pitbull, you need to know some Cuban history.

Cuba is an island nation off the southern coast of Florida. Fulgencio Batista was a military leader there in the 1930s. He was elected president in 1940. He passed laws that gave Cubans more rights than they had in the past. In 1952 he ran for president again. When he knew he would not win the election, he staged a coup and took over the country.

Batista now took away many freedoms from his people. Wealthy Cubans paid Batista for special favors. He allowed American gangsters to do business in Cuba. The gangsters gave money to Batista in return. People started protesting. Batista had the protesters arrested. Some were tortured. Others were killed.

Fidel Castro was one of Batista's opponents. He led attacks against Batista. In 1959 Batista snuck out of Cuba with a fortune. Castro became Cuba's leader.

Castro was a communist, so he changed the laws. All land in Cuba became property of the government. The government controlled the people's activities. People could not choose their career. The government decided how much food and money people would receive. For most, there was not enough of either.

Just like with Batista, people protested Castro's policies. He had them arrested. Thousands of political prisoners were jailed. Many were executed. So people tried to escape Cuba. They took boats or made rafts to sail to Florida. Some made it safely, but many people drowned.

Fidel Castro made Cuba a communist country.

Cuban parents were very worried about their children. Pitbull's grandmother sent her daughter Alysha to the United States in Operation Peter Pan. In this program, the United States took in over 14,000 Cuban children between 1960 and 1962. The children were allowed into the United States, but their parents were not. So Alysha grew up in the United States. She would not see her mother for seven years.

She had more freedoms in the United States than she would have had in Cuba. But she did not have money. She had to learn English. Alysha drank and used drugs, so she could not find good jobs. So she worked in clubs as a dancer.

People continued trying to escape from Cuba. Then in 1980, Cuba and the United States came to an agreement. The United States would take in the Cubans who wanted to leave. Castro agreed to let some Cubans go. Boat after boat arrived in Florida, packed with people. Pitbull's father, Armando Pérez Torrez, brought three boats of people from Cuba to Florida. He brought 547 people to freedom.

When Armando finished the three boat trips to Florida, he stayed there. Armando and Alysha met after he settled in Miami. They had a daughter, Jennifer. On January 15, 1981, Armando Christian Pérez was born. A few years later, they had another daughter, Michelle.

Armando Sr. was proud of his Cuban heritage. He raised his son to have the same pride in his heritage. Armando Sr. taught his son about Cuban poet José Martí. When Armando was three years old, he could recite Martí's poetry.

Pitbull's father brought over 500 people to the United States by boat.

Armando struggled with being both Cuban and American. His parents disagreed about their son's heritage. Armando said, "My mother, she's like, 'Look, you're American, son. You were born here in the States.' My father? My father said, 'You're Cuban American.' My mother would call me Chris, because my middle name's Christian. My father would say, 'No, your name's Armando.'"

Armando Sr. had dreams of selling drugs and making a fortune like he saw in American movies. He became addicted to the drugs he sold and drank too much. By the time Armando was four years old, his parents divorced. Armando Sr. took Michelle with him when he left. Michelle would not see Jennifer and Armando again until she was eighteen years old. Alysha raised Armando and Jennifer alone.

Alysha struggled to raise her children. There were times when they did not have enough food. She could not always afford to pay the electric bill. She struggled with drugs and alcohol. Alysha worked odd jobs when she was able. But when she needed money, she sold their belongings at the pawn shop.

Eventually Alysha could not afford to raise her children. Jennifer was pregnant at age 16. She went to live with relatives. Armando was sent to live in a foster home in Georgia. His white foster family wanted to adopt the blonde, blue-eyed boy. But Armando never felt like he fit in. He wanted his mother. Eventually Alysha had enough money to pay

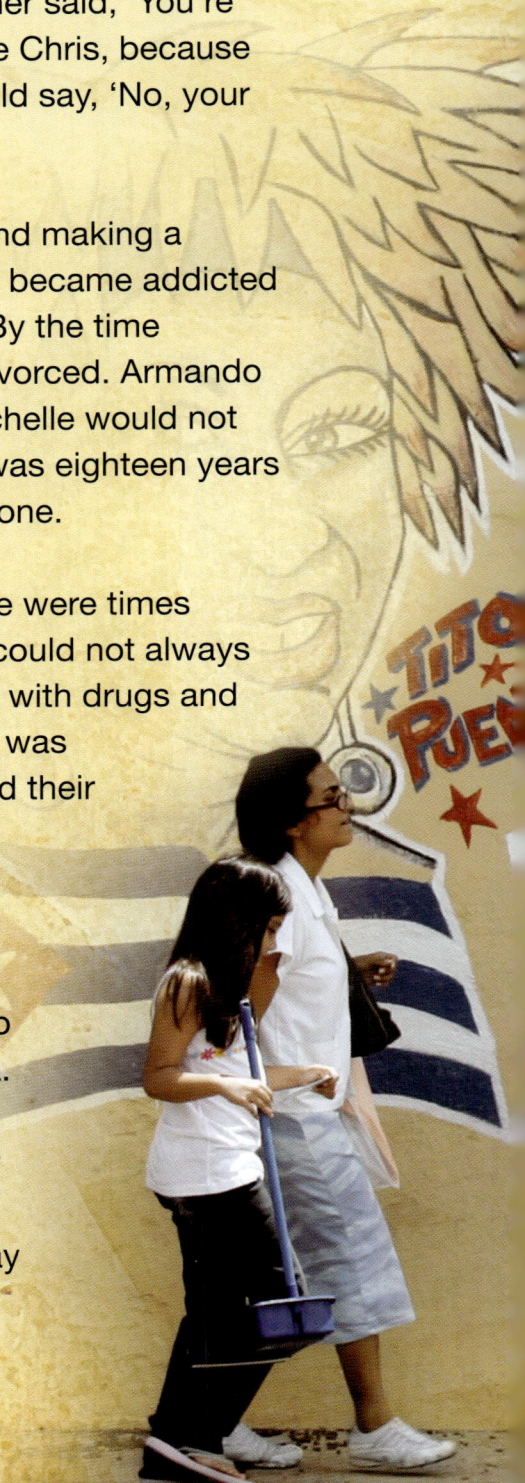

for rent and food. She brought Armando home to Miami. But they would not see Jennifer again for many years.

Armando grew up in Miami where Cuban heritage is strong.

Discovering Rap

Armando discovered rap in his teens. He loved the strong beats. He also liked the power of the words. He would meet friends in the school yard and have freestyle rap battles. They would make up the lyrics as they rapped. Often they would insult each other. Armando was a great freestyler. Crowds of kids would stand around just to hear what he would say.

Kids may have loved Armando's rap on the playground, but he was still poor. So like some teens, Armando started selling drugs. He sold the drugs that kids wanted at rave parties. He was making enough money to buy food and clothes for himself. When his mother found the drugs he was selling, she flushed them down the toilet. This did not stop Armando. He went back to selling drugs because he liked the money too much. When Armando was sixteen years old, his mother was fed up. She said she would not live with another drug dealer. She threw Armando out of the house.

Armando managed to stay in school while he was out of his home. One day the drama teacher saw a crowd on the basketball court. She rushed over because she thought there was a fight. Instead she found Armando rapping. She was so impressed that she got him a part as an extra in rapper DMX's video.

Armando arrived at the video shoot. He did not sit quietly in the background. Instead he got into a freestyle battle with one of DMX's friends, Drag-on. Producer Irv Gotti heard the battle. He congratulated Armando and gave him advice. Freestyling was fun, but there was no money in it. Gotti told Armando to stop freestyling and start writing songs.

Irv Gotti convinced Armando to start writing songs.

Armando took Irv Gotti's advice. He got to work writing raps. He got enough money to pay for recording time. He made copies of his songs and gave them to anyone who would listen.

One person who heard the song was 2 Live Crew's Luther Campbell. He gave Armando advice. If a hip-hop radio station was having a rap battle, he should be there. He should perform at every club that would have him. And Campbell told Armando to put out as many mixtapes as he could afford.

Armando would listen to other artists' songs in clubs and on the radio. If he found a beat he liked, he would take the song to the studio. He would record his rapping over the song. He would make copies of the songs and give them away. This made Armando one of the most popular local rap artists in Miami.

By this time, Armando came up with a new name for himself. He called himself Pitbull. He explained how he and the dog were alike: "They bite to lock. The dog is too stupid to lose. And they're outlawed in Dade County. They're basically everything that I am. It's been a constant fight."

Campbell's advice worked. In 2001 Campbell signed Pitbull to his record label, Luke Records. He gave Pitbull $1,500 for signing the contract. Then he took him on the road. Campbell had Pitbull perform in rap battles during the day and in clubs at night. They toured the South this way, getting Pitbull's music to a bigger audience. Campbell paid Pitbull $210 a week. He sent $180 of it home every week to his mother. His motto was to "Do it for Mom."

Luther Campbell signed Pitbull to Luke Records.

Lil John offered Pitbull a chance to rap on his album.

Pitbull worked very hard, but he did not get the big break he hoped for. Hip-hop fans would look at him and see that he was Latino. He did not look like a typical rapper. So they were not very interested in him. When his one-year contract ended, Luke Records let Pitbull go.

With no contract, Pitbull had no money. So he went back to dealing drugs. His father saw him selling drugs on the street one day. Armando told his son that he had not been a father to him, but he could be a friend. Armando warned Pitbull that selling drugs would only lead to prison or death. Pitbull's father asked if they could have a relationship. He convinced his son to leave drug dealing behind.

Pitbull started working with Robert Fernandez, another music producer. He listened to Pitbull's music and recognized a problem. Fernandez showed him that hit songs that get on the radio have hooks, or catchy phrases that repeat through the song. Some of Pitbull's songs did not use hooks. He wrote other songs with hooks late in the music. Fernandez had Pitbull change his writing style to put hooks in early. This made the songs catchier for the listener. It also made the songs more like music that was on the radio.

Pitbull took one of his new songs to a Miami hip-hop station. The song "Oye" caught the attention of rapper Lil John. Pitbull hoped Lil John would give him a verse or two on his album. Instead, Lil John asked Pitbull to rap an entire song.

Making It Big

Pitbull made a remix of Jermaine Dupri's "Welcome to Atlanta." He rewrote the words and called it "Welcome to Miami." He gave a copy to a radio DJ, and the song was a huge local hit. Bootleggers made copies of the recording and sold them on the streets. Music stores had pictures of him up in the windows.

Lil John thought that Pitbull should stop hiding his Latino roots. Instead Lil John suggested that Pitbull play up his heritage. This meant including more Spanish language and Latino beats in his music.

In 2003 Pitbull finally got national attention. The producers of the movie *2 Fast 2 Furious* heard his music. They paid Pitbull to include "Oye" on the soundtrack to the movie. Then Lil John's *Kings of Crunk* came out. It featured the song "Pitbull's Cuban Rideout." The album reached number two on the *Billboard* hip-hop charts.

The DJs on Miami's hip-hop radio stations knew that Pitbull was going to be a star. DJ Laz Mendez said, "A label takes an artist like Pitbull and puts a million dollars behind him and he's gonna blow."

Pitbull used the advice from everyone who had helped him. He used Luther Campbell's advice to keep his music and face visible in Miami. He followed Robert Fernandez's advice and made his music sound more like songs on the radio. And like Lil John said, Pitbull used more Spanish language and rhythms in his music. And now Pitbull was ready for his first hit.

Pitbull was a hit in his hometown with "Welcome to Miami."

Pitbull wrote a rap about women dancing in clubs. He had been a fan of the Miami club scene since he was a young teen. So his song celebrated the way the women danced. He let Lil John listen to the song. Lil John reacted, "When I heard that, I was like, 'Yo, that's a hit record. We got to put that out.'" Pitbull and Lil John re-recorded the song together. Then they gave the mixtapes to the hip-hop radio stations. He gave them to DJs in dance clubs. Like Lil John predicted, it was a huge hit. The song made it to radio and clubs across the United States.

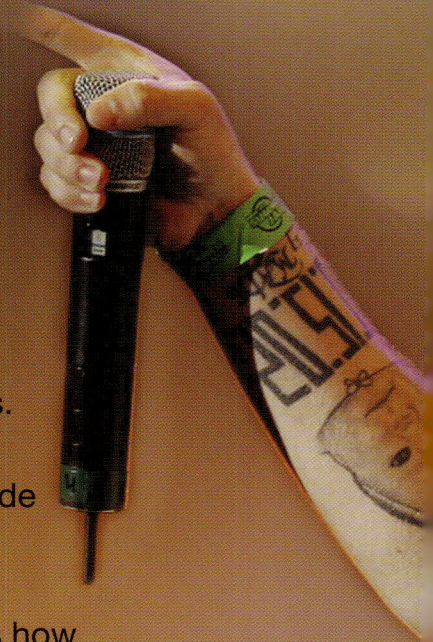

Pitbull was so proud of the hit. He said, "This is how you make a name for yourself with no record deal. No video, no publishing contract. My records climb charts. I'm selling me to the world. I'm not selling gimmicks."

Record companies were finally ready to make a deal with Pitbull. In November 2003 he signed with TVT Records. This was the same company that represented Lil John. They had Lil John help produce his debut album. The album, *M.I.A.M.I.: Money Is a Major Issue*, came out in August 2004.

The album reached number fourteen on the *Billboard* 200 album chart. His first single reached number thirty-two on the *Billboard* Hot 100 chart. The record company released four more songs as singles. The record sold over half a million copies.

Other hip-hop artists liked Pitbull's sound. Eminem and 50 Cent invited Pitbull to join them on their "Anger Management" tour. Pitbull was featured on the Ying Yang Twins' song "Shake." He also performed with Twista on "Hit the Floor."

Pitbull released his first album in 2004.

In 2005 Pitbull formed a new business with Sean "Diddy" Combs and Emilio Estefan. Diddy had a hip-hop record label called Bad Boy Records. He wanted to branch out into the Latino market. Diddy talked to Emilio Estefan, a music producer and member of Miami Sound Machine. (Emilio's wife is Gloria Estefan, the lead singer.) Diddy, Estefan, and Pitbull formed a new record label, Bad Boy Latino.

Their music would blend hip-hop, soul, pop, and Latin music.

Pitbull headed the A&R division. He was responsible for finding new artists. He would work with them to become successful. It was his way of offering the help that artists like Lil John and Luther Campbell gave to him. The company did not start out signing a lot of artists. They were only interested in artists with true talent. According to Estefan, "More than quantity, our interest is in making a major statement."

Pitbull, Emilio Estefan, and Diddy Combs formed Bad Boy Latino Records.

The same year that Bad Boy Latino formed, Pitbull got devastating news. His father, Armando Sr., had liver disease. He would only live for a few more months. Pitbull spent time with his father in the last few months of his life. He tried to keep him happy and comfortable. But Pitbull's career was taking off. He needed to keep working. When Pitbull was on tour in Mexico in May 2006, Armando Sr. died.

Honoring His Father

After his father died, Pitbull worked to honor his memory. He worked with Haitian singer Wyclef Jean and Puerto Rican singers Carlos Ponce and Olga Tañón. The song "Nuestro Himno" was a rewritten version of "The Star Spangled Banner." Their version spoke about the problems of illegal immigrants who come to the United States. It described how families were being torn apart when parents were deported. It also described the immigrants as hard workers who did jobs that nobody else would do. The song was played on hundreds of Spanish-language radio stations.

Some people were very offended by the song. Critics said that the words to the national anthem were sacred. Others disagreed with the song's message. And some people said it was wrong to sing the national anthem in any language other than English.

Pitbull recorded a song about the problems that illegal immigrants face.

George Bush was the president of the United States when the song was released. He said, "I think the national anthem ought to be sung in English, and I think people who want to be a citizen of this country ought to learn English and they ought to learn to sing the national anthem in English."

That statement offended many people. Some pointed out that the anthem had been rewritten many times. There were versions in different languages before this version. Many people pointed out that President Bush spoke Spanish when he visited Latino voters. People called Bush hypocritical.

Pitbull explained his feelings about "Nuestro Himno." He said, "In no way, shape, or form is it disrespecting the national anthem, disrespecting Americans. We're just trying to make a statement You know? For all the people that are trying to come into this country and enjoy America, the United States of America."

President George Bush was offended by Pitbull's song.

25

Pitbul's second album came out in October 2006. *El Mariel* was named for the boatlift that his father took part in. Pitbull dedicated the album to Armando Sr. The music on the album combined the sounds of rap, Latin, and reggaeton. It gave his fans a peek into Pitbull's family history in Cuba. For many it was the first time they learned about the struggles of many Cuban Americans.

Pitbull released the album with lyrics in English and Spanish. He said, "My album is basically a bilingual album. To me it's not only entertaining but it's educating at the same time. When somebody's sitting next to each other and one speaks Spanish and he hears it and he's like, 'Oh.' And then the other one is curious. 'Oh, what did he say, what did he say?' And that's where a bond is created, you know, through fans. That, to me, that's the best part of this music thing right now. That somehow, someway, I've stumbled across a movement where I'm allowed to unify people. You know, and I think that's what's going to be bigger than my music." Pitbull was able to get English-speaking fans to cross over to Latino music. At the same time, he got Latino fans to listen to American hip-hop.

The album also was a mix of radio-style dance hits and more serious songs. He described the story of the Cubans who came to Florida in the 1980s. The album reached number seventeen on the *Billboard* 200 album chart and number two on the rap chart.

Pitbull followed up *El Mariel* with the album *The Boatlift* in 2007. This third album did not sell as well as his previous two.

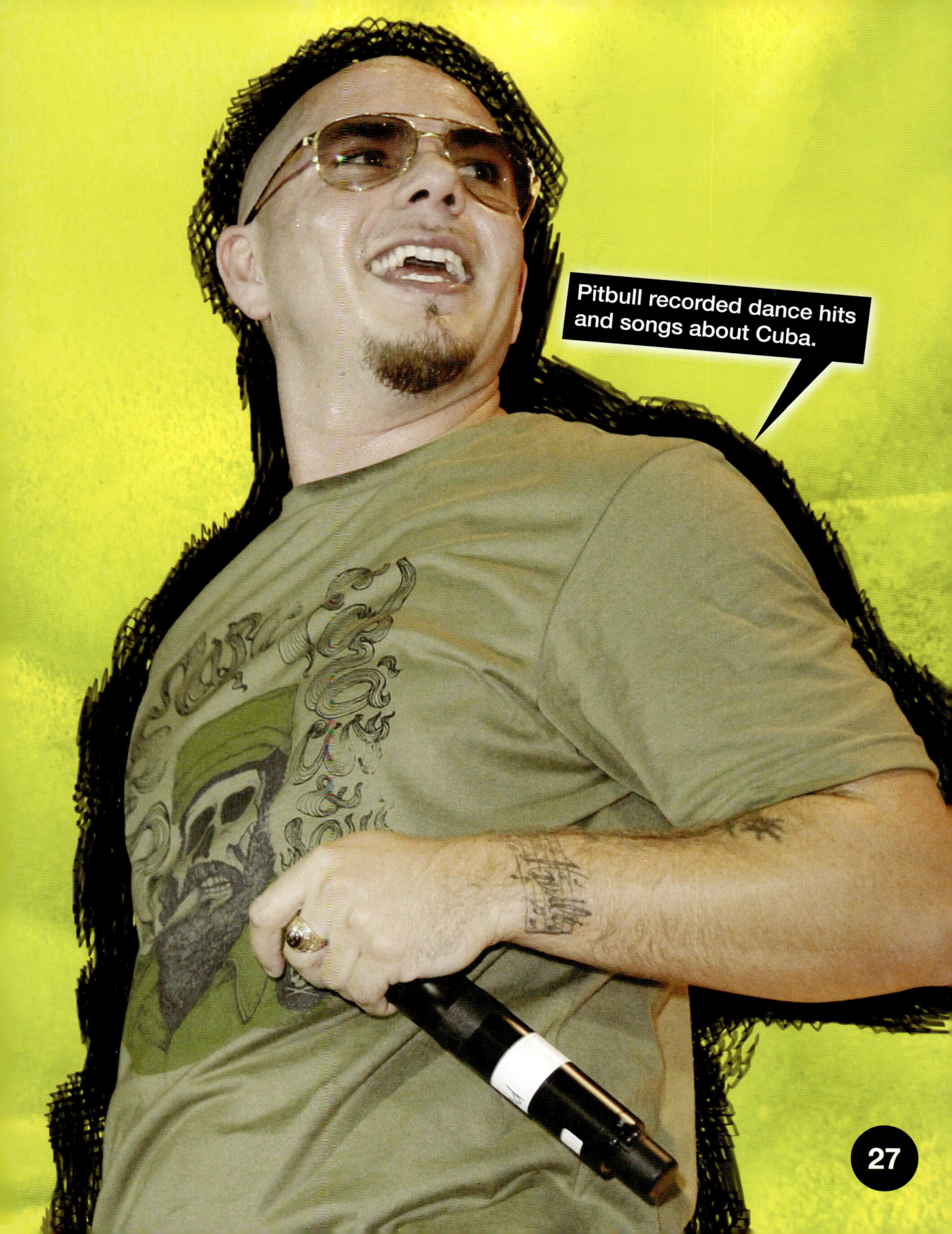

Pitbull recorded dance hits and songs about Cuba.

Branching Out

Pitbull focused on more than just recording his own albums. He was trying to change his image. He gave up his casual T-shirts and jeans. Instead he started performing in polished dress shirts and slacks. He also moved away from hard-core rap to include more party-style music. He also continued to pay respect to his hometown of Miami. The mayor honored him by giving him the key to the city. Pitbull had completely changed his life. He started out as a freestyling drug dealer. Now he was a successful recording artist.

Pitbull also started working in television. He guest starred on the show *South Beach*. It was produced by Jennifer Lopez, another successful Latin singer. The show was not very popular and only lasted a few episodes. But it gave Pitbull some acting experience.

Then he starred in a show called *La Esquina*. The program aired on Telemundo, a Spanish-language network. For two years Pitbull and his partner, Fademaster, pulled pranks and got into funny situations. It also featured other Latin music performers. The show lasted for two years.

During the same two years, Pitbull worked on a project he called "The Invasion." When he first signed his contract with TVT, they limited how many artists he could record with. Now with Bad Boy Latino, he was free to record with anyone he wanted. So Pitbull appeared on records with LMFAO, Rick Ross, DJ Khaled, Flo Rida, and more.

Pitbull starred in his own television show.

Still following Luther Campbell's advice, Pitbull kept making appearances to stay popular. He sang on the video for the Miami Dolphins' fight song with Jimmy Buffet and T-Pain. He was a voice actor in the video game *Scarface: The World Is Yours*. He acted in an Australian movie *From Parts Unknown*. He released many of his songs to appear on television shows and video games. Pitbull also wrote music for the movies *Men in Black II* and *Fast and Furious*.

Pitbull started his own record label, Mr. 305. In 2009 he released his next record. *Rebelution* was his best-selling record to date. It reached number eight on the *Billboard* 200 album chart and number one on the hip-hop chart. He followed up with *Armando*, a Spanish–language album, which he released in 2010. His albums were becoming more and more popular around the world. He was gaining ground not only in the United States, but also worldwide.

Having slow US record sales can be a problem for a recording artist. It can make record companies slow to do business again. But Pitbull was not discouraged.

He said, "Usually the negatives turned out to be the most positive for me. In the music industry, any other artist would have looked at the situation I was in and thought, 'Oh man, this is not for me.' I looked at it more like [Darwin exploring] the Galápagos Islands. You know—survival of the fittest."

Pitbull performed with Enrique Iglesias during a Miami Dolphins football game.

In 2011 Pitbull released his hit album *Planet Pit*. He worked with artists like Chris Brown, Kelly Rowland, Jamie Foxx, Sean Paul, Marc Anthony, and Enrique Iglesias. The single "Give Me Everything" reached the number-one position of the *Billboard* Hot 100 chart. This was Pitbull's first number-one single in his career. The album's success made Pitbull even more in demand. He performed on Jennifer Lopez's "On the Floor." He appeared on the *WWE Monday Night Raw* to celebrate Dwayne "The Rock" Johnson's birthday. He was also invited to perform on the hit late-night show *Conan*.

Four months after the single "Give Me Everything" came out, something very strange happened. The actress Lindsay Lohan sued Pitbull. He mentioned her by name in the song. He also hinted at the fact that she had served time in jail. Lohan was not suing because Pitbull's song was untrue.

She was suing because four words in the song were about her. She was concerned that Pitbull would make money because of her. She wanted the song never to be played again. She had sued a company for $100 million the year before for simply mentioning the name "Lindsay." People thought that she just wanted Pitbull to offer her money to drop the lawsuit.

Pitbull did not offer Lohan a dime. In fact, he fought back. He sued Lohan, saying she was getting in the way of his freedom of speech. He also claimed that Lohan's lawyers copied the information in the lawsuit from someone else. In other words, her lawyer committed plagiarism. So far the two cases have not been settled. But "Give Me Everything" has not stopped playing, either.

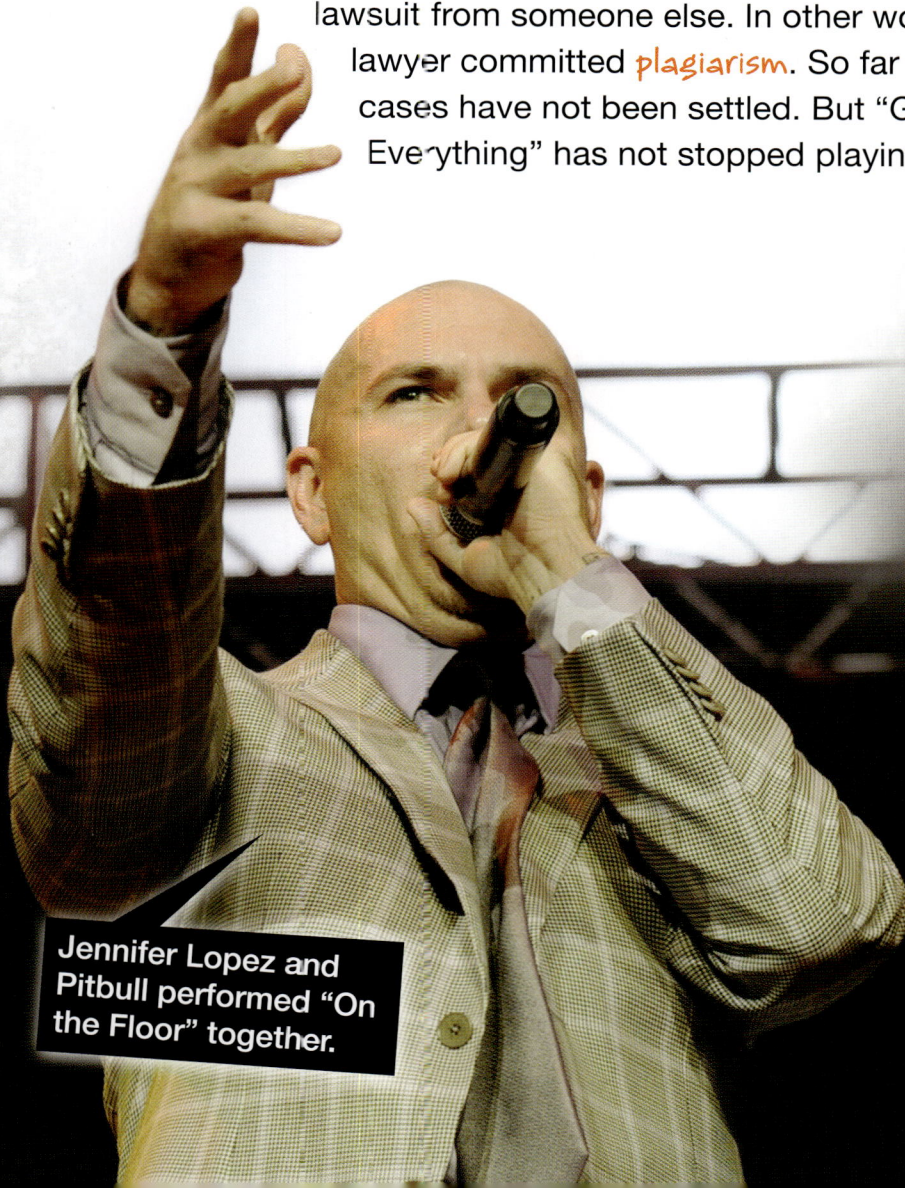

Jennifer Lopez and Pitbull performed "On the Floor" together.

Supporting His Fans

Pitbull's seventh album, *Global Warming*, was released in the fall of 2012. He worked with more stars, including Shakira and Enrique Iglesias. To promote the album, Pitbull went on a world tour. He performed in Mexico, Canada, Europe, Asia, Australia, and the United States.

Pitbull has been very supportive of his fans. He performed in huge cities like Tokyo and Madrid. But he also took the time to perform in small countries like Mongolia. He brought a full laser show to an audience who would rarely see an American singer at all.

A promotion with Walmart showed the world how much Pitbull loves his fans. Walmart held a contest. The store with the most Facebook likes would win an appearance by Pitbull. A writer thought it would be funny to send Pitbull somewhere remote. The writer invited people to vote for the Walmart in the small town of Kodiak, Alaska. Pitbull reacted in a video on his website: "I heard that Kodiak, Alaska, has the most likes due to someone that thinks he was playing a prank … but you've got to understand, I will go anywhere in the world for my fans."

Pitbull lived up to his word. He came to the Kodiak Walmart and greeted the people of the town. He performed at the nearby Coast Guard base. He enjoyed traditional dances by the members of the Alutiiq tribe. And to show what a good sport he was, Pitbull invited the writer who started the prank to join him in Kodiak. They took pictures together before Pitbull returned to his world tour.

Pitbull launched a world tour in 2012 to promote *Global Warming.*

As Pitbull became more popular, businesses wanted him to represent their brands. Kodak chose Pitbull as one of three musicians for their "So Kodak" campaign. Drake, Trey Songz, and Pitbull each had commercials, billboards, magazine ads, and Internet promotions. Each musician's music was featured in the Internet promotions and television commercials. Pitbull said, "As an artist, I have the opportunity to travel and experience the world from a unique point of view. My life is So Kodak, full of hot moments that I want to capture and share with family, friends, and fans."

Pitbull also started working with Daymond John, the founder of FUBU clothing. Pitbull does not want to go into the clothing business. He just wants to be in business. John is one of the entrepreneurs on the television show *Shark Tank*. On the show he invests in businesses that look like they could become successful. John buys a portion of these businesses in exchange for his help in running the business. With John's advice, Pitbull is doing the same thing.

Because Pitbull is popular in so many countries around the world, companies can get an audience in many countries. By following John's example, Pitbull became part owner of a vodka company in exchange for being in their commercials and other ads. In other cases, Pitbull simply gets paid for his work. How does he know how to make the deal? He says, "It all depends on how you look at a deal and break it down. Different deals get struck differently."

Pitbull is also a master of social media. He has millions of Facebook fans. He posts messages and songs on YouTube. He is consistently one of the most-often viewed artists.

Pitbull became a spokesperson for Kodak cameras.

When Pitbull started in hip-hop, his heritage was a problem. He remembered, "I already had three strikes against me. One, I have light skin. Two, I'm from Miami, which wasn't getting looked at the time. Three, I'm Cuban. But now, I've made everything that stacked against me into a virtue." He now sees his background as an advantage. He explains, "It couldn't be a better time for a Hispanic. Because I don't know if anybody looked at the census report. We're the up-and-coming minority, and we're just growing at phenomenal numbers."

Unlike other rappers, Pitbull is not strict about only performing hip-hop. He is willing to include other styles of music on his records. He believes that growing up in Miami made him more willing to include other music. He says, "I grew up around salsa, merengue, bachata, bass music, freestyle, hip-hop, techno, house, rave. Miami is special for that. It's a city where you don't know if it's more a part of the United States, or of the Caribbean, or of Latin America, or of Europe."

Pitbull thinks that fans can relate to the Cuban American struggles he has rapped about. He says, "I just want them to know where I'm from. Just like Jamaicans do, just like Puerto Ricans with Reggaeton. Just like black people with slavery, Jewish with the Holocaust, Cubans and Nicaraguans who had revolutions in their country, so I just want them to know my culture, my struggle, so they can learn from us as much as we learn from them."

Pitbull and Ne-Yo performed on the *Today* show.

No Going Back

Pitbull is proud to call himself a Cuban American. But he is in no hurry to see where his parents grew up. The Cuban government has relaxed some of Fidel Castro's rules. Some people have been allowed to travel in and out of Cuba. But until the government changes, he is staying away. He says, "I won't perform in Cuba until there's no more Castro and there's a free Cuba. To me, Cuba's the biggest prison in the world, and I would be very hypocritical were I to perform there. The people in Cuba, they know what I stand for, and there's a lot of people in Cuba that stand for the same. But they can't say it."

Pitbull compared living in Cuba today to living in a prison.

Other artists have visited Cuba and even performed there. The Columbian singing star Juanes went to Cuba. Pitbull thinks that artists who visit Cuba do not understand the situation. He explains, "I respect him as an artist—he's like U2, the Bono of Spanish. I don't respect his decision. Maybe he doesn't really understand it at the end of the day because he's not Cuban."

Pitbull tries to explain what living in Cuba is still like. He says, "It's almost like being in prison. You can't think. You can't have your own opinions. You have no opportunity. You just gotta live life the way you were born into it. You know, there's no way you can … how can I say it? There's no progress." He knows that many Cubans want to leave and live in the United States but cannot. There are also many Cuban Americans who would like to reunite with family back in Cuba, but they cannot. So until Cuba is free, Pitbull will stay away.

Pitbull works to help immigrant children.

Pitbull supports the rights of immigrants. Many states have passed laws to help identify people who are in the country illegally. Critics claim some of the laws are racist. They could be used to make life harder for Latinos, whether they are legal immigrants or not.

Arizona's immigration bill is very strict. Because Pitbull believes it is unfair, he canceled his shows there. Pitbull explains, "The United States was built by immigrants, so it's very sad. I know everything in life has to have boundaries, rules, and regulations. I agree with that. I don't agree when the USA, that lives by a constitution, says, 'OK, just because you look this way, we're going to ask you for your documentation, or you gotta go back to your country.' The Arizona law is like we took ten steps back … I relate to it, because my family did the same." Pitbull raps about his beliefs. In "Give Me Everything" he says that his family is Cuban, but he is an "American Idol." Pitbull says, "That is me rapping for our people, for anybody who's had to go to another country and develop a whole new life."

Pitbull does not just talk and sing about his support of immigrants. He has started an organization to help immigrant children. His Imaginate Foundation helps start schools that can address the needs of children away from their home countries. He describes the foundation like this: "I want to help others and make them understand that as long as they work hard, as long as they are good people, they can actually make a change in their life no matter where they came from, what obstacles they have to overcome."

Pitbull is also helping teens and young adults understand how important voting is. In Cuba only one candidate runs for any office. The government encourages its people to support the candidate. So there really are no choices in an election. This makes Pitbull appreciate that there are real candidates and real choices in US elections.

In addition, Pitbull was arrested as a teenager. The crime he was charged with was a felony. He was able to get the charge removed from his record. If he had not, he would have lost his right to vote for the rest of his life. Nearly losing his right to vote made a big impact on Pitbull. He says it "definitely made it a whole lot more important to me and made me realize … I wasn't taking advantage of the one right given me being a US citizen."

Many Americans do not vote. If they want to vote, they must register themselves. If they do not know how to register, they will not get the chance to vote. The group Vota Latina helps people get registered. Pitbull made ads showing people how they could use text messaging to register to vote. Vota Latina hopes to get seven million young Latino Americans registered.

Pitbull explains why he works with Vota Latina: "I'm going to vote and I want everybody out there to know it." He continues, "One little vote could change everybody, the whole country's life."

From dance hits in clubs to working to get out the vote, Pitbull is still taking Luther Campbell's advice. He is making his music and messages available for the world to hear.

Pitbull wants to share a positive message with his music.

45

Vocabulary

A&R	(adjective)	Artist and Repertoire; the division of a record company responsible for finding new talent
Billboard	(noun)	magazine that covers the music industry, including record and album sales
bootlegger	(noun)	a person who sells illegal copies of something, like clothes or music
contract	(noun)	an agreement between two people, between two companies, or between a person and a company
critic	(noun)	a person who judges
communist	(noun)	a person who believes that all property and goods should be owned by the government
coup	(noun)	a sudden and successful action
debut	(noun)	someone's first appearance
deport	(verb)	to force someone out of a country
DJ	(noun)	a person who plays records or mixes records, usually at a party or club
execute	(verb)	to put to death
foster home	(noun)	a home where a child can live when family is unable to care for him or her
hip-hop	(adjective or noun)	using strong beats and chanted words; music that uses strong beats and chanted words

hypocritical	(adjective)	acting as if one believes in certain values, but not really holding those values
immigrant	(noun)	a person who moves to a new country to live there
Latino	(adjective)	with Latin-American heritage or background
lyrics	(noun)	words to a song
mixtape	(noun)	a CD of songs made without a record company
political prisoner	(noun)	a person placed in prison for disagreeing with the government
plagiarism	(noun)	the use of someone else's writing as one's own
pop	(adjective or noun)	generally appealing; a watered-down version of rock and roll
producer	(noun)	a person who raises money to create a song, a stage show, and so on
promote	(verb)	to sell or advertise for a product
protest	(noun)	to complain or speak out against
rap	(adjective, verb, or noun)	spoken with rhythm; to speak with rhythm; music in which words are spoken in rhythm
rave	(noun)	a dance party with electronic music, light shows, and often drugs
reggaeton	(noun)	music that combines reggae and urban music
sacred	(adjective)	highly honored
single	(noun)	one song, usually from an album
torture	(verb)	to cause great pain as a form of punishment

Photo Credits

AP Images: Harold Valentine/Associated Press pp. 6–7; Jacques Langevin/Associated Press p. 9; Alan Diaz/Associated Press pp. 10–11; Jim Cooper/Associated Press p. 13; Rich Schultz/Associated Press pp. 20–21; Wilfredo Lee/Associated Press p. 24; James D. Smith/Associated Press pp. 30–31; Arthur Mola/Associated Press pp. 34–35; PR Newswire pp. 36–37; Mitchell Zachs p. 45

Getty Images: Carlos Alvarez/Redferns Cover; Larry Marano/Getty Images Entertainment pp. 4–5; Gustavo Caballero/Getty Images Entertainment p. 15; Vince Bucci/Getty Images Entertainment pp. 16–17; Alexander Tamargo/Getty Images Entertainment p. 19; Paul Hawthorne/Getty Images Entertainment pp. 22–23; Brendan Smialowski/AFP p. 25; John Parra/WireImage p. 27; Alexander Tamargo/Getty Images Entertainment p. 29; Kevin Winter/Getty Images Entertainment pp. 32–33; Michael N. Todaro/Getty Images Entertainment p. 39; Bloomberg pp. 40–41; John Parra/Getty Images Entertainment p. 42